PIKA
Life in the Rocks

TANNIS BILL

Photographs by

JIM JACOBSON

BOYDS MILLS PRESS
Honesdale, Pennsylvania

High in the Rocky Mountains,
a loose pile of rocks lies at the base of a cliff.

Soaking up the sunshine is a pika. His colors
blend with the rocks.

It's time to find food for the winter.
He has found a bush nearby.
He snips the tips off leafy branches.

The pika gathers his food into bundles and carries them in his mouth.

He stacks the bundles under the shelter of a rock. He's building a hay pile.

He hears a noise.
Where is it
coming from?

It's a weasel! Weasels eat pikas! The weasel can stretch out his body and follow a pika into the cracks between the rocks.

The pika stays still.

Finally, the weasel
leaves to hunt mice.

The pika cuts grasses,
berries, flowers, and
leaves. He makes
hundreds of trips each
day, all summer long.

He makes the hay pile
bigger and bigger.

The pika hears a sound.
It might be another pika coming
to steal the food from his hay pile.

The pika makes a warning cry
to scare away the other pika.
"*Eeeeep!*"

"Sniff! Sniff!" His food is safe.

During the fall, the pika keeps adding bundles of plants. The hay pile is as large as a bathtub.

The pika scurries back and forth.
He doesn't know that he is being watched.

Above him, a young hawk is ready
to swoop down. The pika luckily
chooses this moment to rest.
He disappears into a crack among the
rocks and finds a cool, safe place.

Winter is coming. The pika's fur grows thick and warm.

In the winter, the pika doesn't hibernate like a bear. He makes tunnels through the snow to reach his hay pile. Sometimes he pops up from a tunnel to find other plants.

Now the pika's hard work
is paying off. He eats about
nine times a day—grass, leaves,
flowers, berries, and branches.

Some of the plants contain poisons. They last a long time without spoiling. The pika eats the safe plants first and the poisonous plants later in the winter, after most of the poisons are gone.

Before the snow starts to melt, the pika sings a song. Spring will soon be here. He is calling for a mate to start a family.

A female pika stops to listen to his song. The pikas mate. About a month later, the female goes to her nest in her hay pile and has three babies, or pups.

At first, the pups are blind and almost hairless. After three or four weeks, they have opened their eyes and grown some fur. They come out of the rocks for the first time.

The pups stay with their mother
for four more weeks. Then they
move out, and each one finds
a new place to live not far from
home. After three months, they
are as big as their parents.

Now each young pika starts working
to find its own food. Every pika makes
its own hay pile for the winter.
The cycle of another year begins.

The End

ACTUAL SIZE

PIKA FACTS

How to Say *Pika*: PIKE-ah or PEEK-ah

Scientific Name: *Ochotona princeps*

How to Say It: OACH-uh-toh-nuh
(or OAK-uh-toh-nuh) PRIHN-seps

Meaning: "little chief hare." *Ochotona* comes from *ochodona*, the Mongolian word for *pika*. (The animals also live in Asia.) The second term, *princeps*, is Latin for *chief*.

Common Names: American pika, rock rabbit, hay maker, coney, piping hare, whistling hare, mouse hare, little chief hare

Length: 6½ to 8½ inches (162 to 216 millimeters)

Weight: 4 to 6 ounces (121 to 176 grams)

Habitat: Masses of broken rock called talus in cool, moist climates high in the mountains. Pikas may also live in the rocks left over from the mining of precious metals, in lava-flow margins, and occasionally in old house foundations.

Food: Mainly leaves, berries, flowers, and bark from different kinds of plants. Pikas also eat lichens, which are fungi with tiny plants inside, and animal droppings, which are high in protein and calories.

Distribution: Mountains of western North America and Asia. As global climate change has raised temperatures at higher elevations, some pikas have been forced farther up the mountains. Scientists say pikas are losing the habitat they need to survive.

Collared Pika (*Ochotona collaris*)

American Pika (*Ochotona princeps*)

THE PIKA'S FAMILY

Collared Pika

Cottontail Rabbit

Snowshoe Hare

Pikas, rabbits, and hares are not rodents. Instead, they belong to an order of animals called Lagomorpha (lag-oh-MORF-uh), which means "hare shape." Lagomorphs have two pairs of front teeth, or incisors. Mice, rats, squirrels, marmots, and other rodents have only one pair.

Pikas are smaller than rabbits and hares. Pikas also have shorter ears and legs. Scientists think these differences have to do with how these three types of animals survive. The long ears of rabbits and hares are useful for hearing the soft sounds of predators, and their long legs are good for making fast escapes. Long ears also help rabbits and hares get rid of extra body heat. (Blood flows through the ears, where it is cooled by the air.)

The pika's main defense against predators is to dart into the spaces between rocks and hide. It does not need long legs for scurrying through tunnels and among rocks. The pika also listens for predators, but long ears might make hiding a problem. Also, over many years, the pika has adapted to a cool habitat. Its body works in ways that keep body heat, not get rid of it. So small, round ears have worked well for pikas.

Rabbits and hares have short tails, but pikas have no visible tails. No one knows why!

On the soles of their feet, pikas have dense pads of hair, which help them move quietly and efficiently, especially during winter.

PIKA PREDATORS

Weasel
Among all predators, the weasel is the most serious threat to pikas. The weasel can stretch out its body and fit through the cracks between the rocks where the pikas live. Because it does not hibernate or migrate, the weasel is a year-round threat to pikas. The weasel is thought to be more active in the daytime during the summer than in winter, so pikas must always be on the lookout while they gather food on summer days.

Great Horned Owl
The great horned owl is a major nighttime predator of pikas during the spring, summer, and autumn. The pika doesn't have to watch out for the great horned owl during the winter, after the owl has migrated south.

Red Fox
The red fox is a year-round predator of pikas. The fox can curl up, using its tail to keep warm during cold weather. The fox is less of a threat to pikas during the winter, when pikas travel mainly through their snow tunnels.

Northern Hawk Owl
The northern hawk owl is a year-round predator of pikas and hunts both day and night. It uses its keen eyes and ears to find pikas hiding under the snow.

Pine Marten
The pine marten hunts mainly at night throughout the year. Its feet stay warm in the snow because the soles are covered in thick fur.

FOR FURTHER INFORMATION

Books

Miller, Sara Swan. *Rabbits, Pikas, and Hares.* New York: Franklin Watts, 2002.

Orr, Robert T. *The Little-Known Pika.* New York: Macmillan, 1977.

Web Sites*

BBC. Science & Nature Homepage. Animals. North American Pika.
www.bbc.co.uk/nature/wildfacts/factfiles/610.shtml

National Geographic. *National Geographic News.* "Hamster-like Pika in Peril."
news.nationalgeographic.com/news/2009/09/090904-pika-in-peril-missions-video-wc.html

Naturesongs.com. "Other Animal Sounds." Pika's warning call.
www.naturesongs.com/otheranimals.html#pika
(Click on the word "Pikas.")

Pika Works
www.pikaworks.com/pikas/what.html

Smith, Andrew. "The Art of Making Hay—Winter Food-Storing Behavior of the Pika, a Small Mammal." *National Wildlife,* April–May 1997.
findarticles.com/p/articles/mi_m1169/is_n3_v35/ai_19246525/

A pika stretches.

More About the Pika

Pikas have a slit between their upper lips and nostrils called a "hare lip." They have large incisors (front teeth), which they use for ripping leaves and branches off plants and bushes. Pikas' incisors never stop growing, so the animals need to wear them down constantly.

Author's Note to Older Readers

Scientists who study pikas predict that many populations of these mammals will become extirpated as a consequence of global climate change. As temperatures increase, pikas, which require cool, moist habitats, are being forced to move to higher mountain habitats to find suitable places to live. Warmer temperatures are making the pikas' food ripen earlier in the year. While pikas gather their winter's supply of food in the heat, their bodies are stressed from wearing their heavy winter coats. Scientists think that, in time, higher temperatures will reach the mountaintops and there will be insufficient habitat for pikas to survive.

In late 2007, the Center for Biological Diversity unsuccessfully petitioned the California Fish and Game Commission to list pikas as an endangered species in the state. In 2009, the commission received a court order to reconsider the decision. In addition, the U.S. Fish and Wildlife Service has begun a review of the pika's status nationally. That review was scheduled to result in a decision by February 1, 2010, whether to protect pikas under the U.S. Endangered Species Act by 2011. By the time you read this book, the decisions may have been made.

The following are Web-based resources related to this issue. These Web sites were active at the time this book was published.

Center for Biological Diversity
www.biologicaldiversity.org/species/mammals/American_pika/index.html

Petition to the U.S. Fish and Wildlife Service
www.fws.gov/mountain-prairie/species/mammals/americanpika/AmericanPikaPetition10012007.pdf

World Wildlife Federation. "Impact of Climate Change on the American Pika."
www.panda.org/about_our_earth/aboutcc/problems/impacts/species/pikas/

PIKA WORDS

camouflage a color or pattern of colors in an animal's fur, feathers, scales, or skin that helps the animal hide by blending into the environment. When a pika sits still until a predator leaves, the pika is using its camouflage to avoid detection.

carnivore an animal that eats mainly meat. Predators such as hawks and weasels are carnivores.

herbivore an animal that eats mainly plants. Pikas are herbivores.

molt to shed all or part of an outer covering, allowing new growth. A pika sheds hair when it molts. Other animals shed feathers, scales, or their entire outer skin.

predator an animal that eats other animals. See page 30 for predators that hunt pikas.

preservative a chemical that prevents food from decaying or spoiling. The poisons in some plants in a pika's hay pile act as preservatives and keep the plants from spoiling.

prey an animal that is eaten by other animals. Some pikas become the prey of other animals.

talus a pile or slope of rocks that have broken off and fallen to the base of a cliff. The pika lives in talus.

vocalize to express something using the voice. When a male pika warns away other pikas or sings for a mate, he is vocalizing.

Acknowledgments

We have many people to thank for their help in making this book possible: our families and friends for their support and encouragement; the author's husband, Duane Bill, for his computer expertise; and the author's daughter, Shannon Dunlop, an elementary-school teacher, for editing the manuscript. We would like to thank our editor, Andy Boyles, for his patience and expertise.

We dedicate this book to Dr. Erik Beever, an ecologist who has studied pikas for more than fifteen years. Dr. Beever has reviewed the manuscript and taught us all so much about pikas.
—T.B. and J.J.

Image Credits

Page 28: map by Derek F. Williams, 2009, and Environmental Systems Research Institute, Inc., 2004 (based on Smith, A.T., and M. L. Weston. 1990. *Ochotona princeps. Mammalian Species.* 352:1–8; and MacDonald, S. O., and C. Jones. 1987. *Ochotona collaris. Mammalian Species.* 281:1–4.)

Page 29: collared pika by Mark A. Chappell; cottontail rabbit © Robert Shantz/Alamy; snowshoe hare © Photoshot Holdings Ltd./Alamy.

Boyds Mills Press, Inc.
815 Church Street
Honesdale, Pennsylvania 18431
Printed in the United States of America

CIP data is available.

First edition
The text of this book is set in 24-point Gil Sans.

10 9 8 7 6 5 4 3 2 1